THE BLUEST EYE

Toni Morrison

This edition published by Spark Publishing

Spark Publishing
A Division of SparkNotes LLC
120 Fifth Avenue, 8th Floor
New York, NY 10011

Printed and bound in the United States

ISBN ISBN 1-58663-501-8

Introduction:
Stopping to Buy Sparknotes on a Snowy Evening

Whose words these are you *think* you know.
Your paper's due tomorrow, though;
We're glad to see you stopping here
To get some help before you go.

Lost your course? You'll find it here.
Face tests and essays without fear.
Between the words, good grades at stake:
Get great results throughout the year.

Once school bells caused your heart to quake
As teachers circled each mistake.
Use SparkNotes and no longer weep,
Ace every single test you take.

Yes, books are lovely, dark, and deep,
But only what you grasp you keep,
With hours to go before you sleep,
With hours to go before you sleep.

CONTENTS

CONTEXT

ONI MORRISON WAS BORN Chloe Anthony Wofford in 1931 in Lorain, Ohio. Her mother's family had come to Ohio from Alabama via Kentucky, and her father had migrated from Georgia. Morrison grew up with a love of literature and received her undergraduate degree from Howard University. She received a master's degree from Cornell University, completing a thesis on William Faulkner and Virginia Woolf. Afterward, she taught at Texas Southern University and then at Howard, in Washington, D.C., where she met Harold Morrison, an architect from Jamaica. The marriage lasted six years, and Morrison gave birth to two sons. She and her husband divorced while she was pregnant with her second son, and she returned to Lorain to give birth. She then moved to New York and became an editor at Random House, specializing in black fiction. During this difficult and somewhat lonely time, she began working on her first novel, *The Bluest Eye,* which was published in 1970.

Morrison's first novel was not an immediate success, but she continued to write. *Sula,* which appeared in 1973, was more successful, earning a nomination for the National Book Award. In 1977, *Song of Solomon* launched Morrison's national reputation, winning her the National Book Critics' Circle Award. Her most well-known work, *Beloved,* appeared in 1987 and won the Pulitzer Prize. Her other novels include *Tar Baby* (1981), *Jazz* (1992), and *Paradise* (1998). Meanwhile, Morrison returned to teaching and was a professor at Yale and the State University of New York at Albany. Today, she is the Robert F. Goheen Professor in the Council of Humanities at Princeton University, where she teaches creative writing. In 1993, Morrison became the first African-American woman to receive the Nobel Prize in literature.

The Bluest Eye contains a number of autobiographical elements. It is set in the town where Morrison grew up, and it is told from the point of view of a nine-year-old, the age Morrison would have been the year the novel takes place (1941). Like the MacTeer family, Morrison's family struggled to make ends meet during the Great Depression. Morrison grew up listening to her mother singing and her grandfather playing the violin, just as Claudia does. In the novel's afterword, Morrison explains that the story developed out of a conversation she had had in elementary school with a little girl, who longed for blue eyes. She was still thinking about this conversation in the 1960s, when the Black is Beautiful movement was working to reclaim African-American beauty, and she began her first novel.

While its historical context is clear, the literary context of *The Bluest Eye* is more complex. Faulkner and Woolf, whose work Morrison knew well, influenced her style. She uses the modernist techniques of stream-of-consciousness, multiple perspectives, and deliberate fragmentation. But Morrison understands her work more fundamentally as part of a black cultural tradition and strives to create a distinctively black literature. Her prose is infused with black musical traditions such as the spirituals, gospel, jazz and the blues. She writes in a black vernacular, full of turns of phrase and figures of speech unique to the community in which she grew up, with the hope that if she is true to her own particular experience, it will be universally meaningful. In this way, she attempts to create what she calls a "race-specific yet race-free prose."

In the afterword to *The Bluest Eye*, Morrison explains her goal in writing the novel. She wants to make a statement about the damage that internalized racism can do to the most vulnerable member of a community—a young girl. At the same time, she does not want to dehumanize the people who wound this girl, because that would simply repeat their mistake. Also, she wants to protect this girl from "the weight of the novel's inquiry," and thus decides to tell the story from multiple perspectives. In this way, as she puts it, she "shape[s] a silence while breaking it," keeping the girl's dignity intact.

Plot Overview

NINE-YEAR-OLD CLAUDIA and ten-year-old Frieda MacTeer live in Lorain, Ohio, with their parents. It is the end of the Great Depression, and the girls' parents are more concerned with making ends meet than with lavishing attention upon their daughters, but there is an undercurrent of love and stability in their home. The MacTeers take in a boarder, Henry Washington, and also a young girl named Pecola. Pecola's father has tried to burn down his family's house, and Claudia and Frieda feel sorry for her. Pecola loves Shirley Temple, believing that whiteness is beautiful and that she is ugly.

Pecola moves back in with her family, and her life is difficult. Her father drinks, her mother is distant, and the two of them often beat one another. Her brother, Sammy, frequently runs away. Pecola believes that if she had blue eyes, she would be loved and her life would be transformed. Meanwhile, she continually receives confirmation of her own sense of ugliness—the grocer looks right through her when she buys candy, boys make fun of her, and a light-skinned girl, Maureen, who temporarily befriends her makes fun of her too. She is wrongly blamed for killing a boy's cat and is called a "nasty little black bitch" by his mother.

We learn that Pecola's parents have both had difficult lives. Pauline, her mother, has a lame foot and has always felt isolated. She loses herself in movies, which reaffirm her belief that she is ugly and that romantic love is reserved for the beautiful. She encourages her husband's violent behavior in order to reinforce her own role as a martyr. She feels most alive when she is at work, cleaning a white woman's home. She loves this home and despises her own. Cholly, Pecola's father, was abandoned by his parents and raised by his great aunt, who died when he was a young teenager. He was humiliated by two white men who found him having sex for the first time and made him continue while they watched. He ran away to find his father but was rebuffed by him. By the time he met Pauline, he was a wild and rootless man. He feels trapped in his marriage and has lost interest in life.

Cholly returns home one day and finds Pecola washing dishes. With mixed motives of tenderness and hatred that are fueled by guilt, he rapes her. When Pecola's mother finds her unconscious on the floor, she disbelieves Pecola's story and beats her. Pecola goes to Soaphead Church, a sham mystic, and asks him for blue eyes. Instead of helping her, he uses her to kill a dog he dislikes.

Claudia and Frieda find out that Pecola has been impregnated by her father, and unlike the rest of the neighborhood, they want the baby to live. They sacrifice the money they have been saving for a bicycle and plant marigold seeds. They believe that if the flowers live, so will Pecola's baby. The flowers refuse to bloom, and Pecola's baby dies when it is born prematurely. Cholly, who rapes Pecola a second time and then runs away, dies in a workhouse. Pecola goes mad, believing that her cherished wish has been fulfilled and that she has the bluest eyes.

CHARACTER LIST

Pecola Breedlove The protagonist of the novel, an eleven-year-
old black girl who believes that she is ugly and that
having blue eyes would make her beautiful. Sensitive
and delicate, she passively suffers the abuse of her
mother, father, and classmates. She is lonely and
imaginative.

Claudia MacTeer The narrator of parts of the novel. An
independent and strong-minded nine-year-old, Claudia
is a fighter and rebels against adults' tyranny over
children and against the black community's
idealization of white beauty standards. She has not yet
learned the self-hatred that plagues her peers.

Cholly Breedlove Pecola's father, who is impulsive and violent—
free, but in a dangerous way. Having suffered early
humiliations, he takes out his frustration on the women
in his life. He is capable of both tenderness and rage,
but as the story unfolds, rage increasingly dominates.

Pauline (Polly) Breedlove Pecola's mother, who believes that
she is ugly; this belief has made her lonely and cold. She
has a deformed foot and sees herself as the martyr of a
terrible marriage. She finds meaning not in her own
family but in romantic movies and in her work caring
for a well-to-do white family.

Frieda MacTeer Claudia's ten-year-old sister, who shares
Claudia's independence and stubbornness. Because she
is closer to adolescence, Frieda is more vulnerable to
her community's equation of whiteness with beauty.
Frieda is more knowledgeable about the adult world
and sometimes braver than Claudia.

Mrs. MacTeer Claudia's mother, an authoritarian and sometimes callous woman who nonetheless steadfastly loves and protects her children. She is given to fussing aloud and to singing the blues.

Mr. MacTeer Claudia's father, who works hard to keep the family fed and clothed. He is fiercely protective of his daughters.

Henry Washington The MacTeers' boarder, who has a reputation for being a steady worker and a quiet man. Middle-aged, he has never married and has a lecherous side.

Sammy Breedlove Pecola's fourteen-year-old brother, who copes with his family's problems by running away from home. His active response contrasts with Pecola's passivity.

China, Poland, Miss Marie The local whores, Miss Marie (also known as the Maginot Line) is fat and affectionate, China is skinny and sarcastic, and Poland is quiet. They live above the Breedlove apartment and befriend Pecola.

Mr. Yacobowski The local grocer, a middle-aged white immigrant. He has a gruff manner toward little black girls.

Rosemary Villanucci A white, comparatively wealthy girl who lives next door to the MacTeers. She makes fun of Claudia and Frieda and tries to get them into trouble, and they sometimes beat her up.

Maureen Peal A light-skinned, wealthy black girl who is new at the local school. She accepts everyone else's assumption that she is superior and is capable of both generosity and cruelty.

Geraldine A middle-class black woman who, though she keeps house flawlessly and diligently cares for the physical appearances of herself and her family (including her husband, Louis, and her son, Junior), is essentially cold. She feels real affection only for her cat.

Junior Geraldine's son, who, in the absence of genuine affection from his mother, becomes cruel and sadistic. He tortures the family cat and harasses children who come to the nearby playground.

Soaphead Church Born Elihue Micah Whitcomb, he is a light-skinned West Indian misanthrope and self-declared "Reader, Adviser, and Interpreter of Dreams." He hates all kinds of human touch, with the exception of the bodies of young girls. He is a religious hypocrite.

Aunt Jimmy The elderly woman who raises Cholly. She is affectionate but physically in decay.

Samson Fuller Cholly's father, who abandoned Cholly's mother when she got pregnant. He lives in Macon, Georgia, and is short, balding, and mean.

Blue Jack A co-worker and friend of Cholly's during his boyhood. He is a kind man and excellent storyteller.

M'Dear A quiet, elderly woman who serves as a doctor in the community where Cholly grows up. She is tall and impressive, and she carries a hickory stick.

Darlene The first girl that Cholly likes. She is pretty, playful and affectionate.

ANALYSIS OF MAJOR CHARACTERS

PECOLA BREEDLOVE

Pecola is the protagonist of *The Bluest Eye,* but despite this central role she is passive and remains a mysterious character. Morrison explains in her novel's afterword that she purposely tells Pecola's story from other points of view to keep Pecola's dignity and, to some extent, her mystery intact. She wishes to prevent us from labeling Pecola or prematurely believing that we understand her. Pecola is a fragile and delicate child when the novel begins, and by the novel's close, she has been almost completely destroyed by violence. At the beginning of the novel, two desires form the basis of her emotional life: first, she wants to learn how to get people to love her; second, when forced to witness her parents' brutal fights, she simply wants to disappear. Neither wish is granted, and Pecola is forced further and further into her fantasy world, which is her only defense against the pain of her existence. She believes that being granted the blue eyes that she wishes for would change both how others see her and what she is forced to see. At the novel's end, she delusively believes that her wish has been granted, but only at the cost of her sanity. Pecola's fate is a fate worse than death because she is not allowed any release from her world—she simply moves to "the edge of town, where you can see her even now."

Pecola is also a symbol of the black community's self-hatred and belief in its own ugliness. Others in the community, including her mother, father, and Geraldine, act out their own self-hatred by expressing hatred toward her. At the end of the novel, we are told that Pecola has been a scapegoat for the entire community. Her ugliness has made them feel beautiful, her suffering has made them feel comparatively lucky, and her silence has given them the opportunity for speaking. But because she continues to live after she has lost her mind, Pecola's aimless wandering at the edge of town haunts the community, reminding them of the ugliness and hatred that they have tried to repress. She becomes a reminder of human cruelty and an emblem of human suffering.

CLAUDIA MACTEER

Claudia narrates parts of *The Bluest Eye,* sometimes from a child's perspective and sometimes from the perspective of an adult looking back. Like Pecola, Claudia suffers from racist beauty standards and material insecurity, but she has a loving and stable family, which makes all the difference for her. Whereas Pecola is passive when she is abused, Claudia is a fighter. When Claudia is given a white doll she does not want, she dissects and destroys it. When she finds a group of boys harassing Pecola, she attacks them. When she learns that Pecola is pregnant, she and her sister come up with a plan to save Pecola's baby from the community's rejection. Claudia explains that she is brave because she has not yet learned her limita-tions—most important, she has not learned the self-hatred that plagues so many adults in the community.

Claudia is a valuable guide to the events that unfold in Lorain because her life is stable enough to permit her to see clearly. Her vision is not blurred by the pain that eventually drives Pecola into madness. Her presence in the novel reminds us that most black fam-ilies are not like Pecola's; most black families pull together in the face of hardship instead of fall apart. Claudia's perspective is also valuable because it melds the child's and the adult's points of view. Her childish viewpoint makes her uniquely qualified to register what Pecola experiences, but her adult viewpoint can correct the childish one when it is incomplete. She is a messenger of suffering but also of hope.

CHOLLY BREEDLOVE

By all rights, we should hate Cholly Breedlove, given that he rapes his daughter. But Morrison explains in her afterword that she did not want to dehumanize her characters, even those who dehuman-ize one another, and she succeeds in making Cholly a sympathetic figure. He has experienced genuine suffering, having been aban-doned in a junk heap as a baby and having suffered humiliation at the hands of white men. He is also capable of pleasure and even joy, in the experience of eating a watermelon or touching a girl for the first time. He is capable of violence, but he is also vulnerable, as when two white men violate him by forcing him to perform sexually for their amusement and when he defecates in his pants after encountering his father. Cholly represents a negative form of freedom. He is not free to love and be loved or to enjoy full dignity, but he is free to have sex and fight and even kill; he is free to be indifferent to death. He falls apart when this freedom becomes a complete lack of interest in life, and he reaches for his daughter to remind himself that he is alive.

PAULINE BREEDLOVE

Like Cholly, Pauline inflicts a great deal of pain on her daughter but Morrison nevertheless renders her sympathetically. She experiences more subtle forms of humiliation than Cholly does—her lame foot convinces her that she is doomed to isolation, and the snobbery of the city women in Lorain condemns her to loneliness. In this state, she is especially vulnerable to the messages conveyed by white culture—that white beauty and possessions are the way to happiness. Once, at the movies, she fixes her hair like the white sex symbol Jean Harlow and loses her tooth while eating candy. Though her fantasy of being like Harlow is a failure, Pauline finds another fantasy world—the white household for which she cares. This fantasy world is more practical than her imitation of Hollywood actresses and is more socially sanctioned than the madness of Pecola's fantasy world, but it is just as effective in separating her from the people— her family—she should love. In a sense, Pauline's existence is just as haunted and delusional as her daughter's.

THEMES, MOTIFS & SYMBOLS

THEMES

Themes are the fundamental and often universal ideas explored in a literary work.

WHITENESS AS THE STANDARD OF BEAUTY

The Bluest Eye provides an extended depiction of the ways in which internalized white beauty standards deform the lives of black girls and women. Implicit messages that whiteness is superior are everywhere, including the white baby doll given to Claudia, the idealization of Shirley Temple, the consensus that light-skinned Maureen is cuter than the other black girls, the idealization of white beauty in the movies, and Pauline Breedlove's preference for the little white girl she works for over her daughter. Adult women, having learned to hate the blackness of their own bodies, take this hatred out on their children—Mrs. Breedlove shares the conviction that Pecola is ugly, and lighter-skinned Geraldine curses Pecola's blackness. Claudia remains free from this worship of whiteness, imagining Pecola's unborn baby as beautiful in its blackness. But it is hinted that once Claudia reaches adolescence, she too will learn to hate herself, as if racial self-loathing were a necessary part of maturation.

The person who suffers most from white beauty standards is, of course, Pecola. She connects beauty with being loved and believes that if she possesses blue eyes, the cruelty in her life will be replaced by affection and respect. This hopeless desire leads ultimately to madness, suggesting that the fulfillment of the wish for white beauty may be even more tragic than the wish impulse itself.

SEEING VERSUS BEING SEEN

Pecola's desire for blue eyes, while highly unrealistic, is based on one correct insight into her world: she believes that the cruelty she witnesses and experiences is connected to how she is seen. If she had beautiful blue eyes, Pecola imagines, people would not want to do ugly things in front of her or to her. The accuracy of this insight is affirmed by her experience of being teased by the boys—when Maureen comes to her rescue, it seems that they no longer want to behave badly under Maureen's attractive gaze. In a more basic sense, Pecola and her family are mistreated in part because they happen to have black skin. By wishing for blue eyes rather than lighter skin, Pecola indicates that she wishes to see things differently as much as she wishes to be seen differently. She can only receive this wish, in effect, by blinding herself. Pecola is then able to see herself as beautiful, but only at the cost of her ability to see accurately both herself and the world around her. The connection between how one is seen and what one sees has a uniquely tragic outcome for her.

THE POWER OF STORIES

The Bluest Eye is not one story, but multiple, sometimes contradictory, interlocking stories. Characters tell stories to make sense of their lives, and these stories have tremendous power for both good and evil. Claudia's stories, in particular, stand out for their affirmative power. First and foremost, she tells Pecola's story, and though she questions the accuracy and meaning of her version, to some degree her attention and care redeem the ugliness of Pecola's life. Furthermore, when the adults describe Pecola's pregnancy and hope that the baby dies, Claudia and Frieda attempt to rewrite this story as a hopeful one, casting themselves as saviors. Finally, Claudia resists the premise of white superiority, writing her own story about the beauty of blackness. Stories by other characters are often destructive to themselves and others. The story Pauline Breedlove tells herself about her own ugliness reinforces her self-hatred, and the story she tells herself about her own martyrdom reinforces her cruelty toward her family. Soaphead Church's personal narratives about his good intentions and his special relationship with God are pure hypocrisy. Stories are as likely to distort the truth as they are to reveal it. While Morrison apparently believes that stories can be redeeming, she is no blind optimist and refuses to let us rest comfortably in any one version of what happens.

SEXUAL INITIATION AND ABUSE

To a large degree, *The Bluest Eye* is about both the pleasures and the perils of sexual initiation. Early in the novel, Pecola has her first menstrual period, and toward the novel's end she has her first sexual experience, which is violent. Frieda knows about and anticipates menstruating, and she is initiated into sexual experience when she is fondled by Henry Washington. We are told the story of Cholly's first sexual experience, which ends when two white men force him to finish having sex while they watch. The fact that all of these experiences are humiliating and hurtful indicates that sexual coming-of-age is fraught with peril, especially in an abusive environment.

In the novel, parents carry much of the blame for their children's often traumatic sexual coming-of-age. The most blatant case is Cholly's rape of his own daughter, Pecola, which is, in a sense, a repetition of the sexual humiliation Cholly experienced under the gaze of two racist whites. Frieda's experience is less painful than Pecola's because her parents immediately come to her rescue, playing the appropriate protector and underlining, by way of contrast, the extent of Cholly's crime against his daughter. But Frieda is not given information that lets her understand what has happened to her. Instead, she lives with a vague fear of being "ruined" like the local prostitutes. The prevalence of sexual violence in the novel suggests that racism is not the only thing that distorts black girlhoods. There is also a pervasive assumption that women's bodies are available for abuse. The refusal on the part of parents to teach their girls about sexuality makes the girls' transition into sexual maturity difficult.

Satisfying Appetites versus Suppressing Them

A number of characters in *The Bluest Eye* define their lives through a denial of their bodily needs. Geraldine prefers cleanliness and order to the messiness of sex, and she is emotionally frigid as a result. Similarly, Pauline prefers cleaning and organizing the home of her white employers to expressing physical affection toward her family. Soaphead Church finds physicality distasteful, and this peculiarity leads to his preference for objects over humans and to his perverse attraction to little girls. In contrast, when characters experience happiness, it is generally in viscerally physical terms. Claudia prefers to have her senses indulged by wonderful scents, sounds, and tastes than to be given a hard white doll. Cholly's greatest moments of happinesses are eating the best part of a watermelon and touching a girl for the first time. Pauline's happiest memory is of sexual fulfillment with her husband. The novel suggests that, no matter how messy and sometimes violent human desire is, it is also the source of happiness: denial of the body begets hatred and violence, not redemption.

THEMES

MOTIFS

Motifs are recurring structures, contrasts, or literary devices that can help to develop and inform the text's major themes.

THE DICK-AND-JANE NARRATIVE

The novel opens with a narrative from a Dick-and-Jane reading primer, a narrative that is distorted when Morrison runs its sentences and then its words together. The gap between the idealized, sanitized, upper-middle-class world of Dick and Jane (who we *assume* to be white, though we are never told so) and the often dark and ugly world of the novel is emphasized by the chapter headings excerpted from the primer. But Morrison does not mean for us to think that the Dick-and-Jane world is better—in fact, it is largely because the black characters have internalized white Dick-and-Jane values that they are unhappy. In this way, the Dick and Jane narrative and the novel provide ironic commentary on each other.

THE SEASONS AND NATURE

The novel is divided into the four seasons, but it pointedly refuses to meet the expectations of these seasons. For example, spring, the traditional time of rebirth and renewal, reminds Claudia of being whipped with new switches, and it is the season when Pecola's is raped. Pecola's baby dies in autumn, the season of harvesting. Morrison uses natural cycles to underline the unnaturalness and misery of her characters' experiences. To some degree, she also questions the benevolence of nature, as when Claudia wonders whether "the earth itself might have been unyielding" to someone like Pecola.

WHITENESS AND COLOR

In the novel, whiteness is associated with beauty and cleanliness (particularly according to Geraldine and Mrs. Breedlove), but also with sterility. In contrast, color is associated with happiness, most clearly in the rainbow of yellow, green, and purple memories Pauline Breedlove sees when making love with Cholly. Morrison uses this imagery to emphasize the destructiveness of the black community's privileging of whiteness and to suggest that vibrant color, rather than the pure absence of color, is a stronger image of happiness and freedom.

EYES AND VISION

Pecola is obsessed with having blue eyes because she believes that this mark of conventional, white beauty will change the way that she is seen and therefore the way that she sees the world. There are continual references to other characters' eyes as well—for example, Mr. Yacobowski's hostility to Pecola resides in the blankness in his own eyes, as well as in his inability to see a black girl. This motif underlines the novel's repeated concern for the difference between how we see and how we are seen, and the difference between superficial sight and true insight.

DIRTINESS AND CLEANLINESS

The black characters in the novel who have internalized white, middle-class values are obsessed with cleanliness. Geraldine and Mrs. Breedlove are excessively concerned with housecleaning—though Mrs. Breedlove cleans only the house of her white employers, as if the Breedlove apartment is beyond her help. This fixation on cleanliness extends into the women's moral and emotional quests for purity, but the obsession with domestic and moral sanitation leads them to cruel coldness. In contrast, one mark of Claudia's strength of character is her pleasure in her own dirt, a pleasure that represents self-confidence and a correct understanding of the nature of happiness.

SYMBOLS

Symbols are objects, characters, figures, or colors used to represent abstract ideas or concepts.

THE HOUSE

The novel begins with a sentence from a Dick-and-Jane narrative: "Here is the house." Homes not only indicate socioeconomic status in this novel, but they also symbolize the emotional situations and values of the characters who inhabit them. The Breedlove apartment is miserable and decrepit, suffering from Mrs. Breedlove's preference for her employer's home over her own and symbolizing the misery of the Breedlove family. The MacTeer house is drafty and dark, but it is carefully tended by Mrs. MacTeer and, according to Claudia, filled with love, symbolizing that family's comparative cohesion.

BLUEST EYE(S)

To Pecola, blue eyes symbolize the beauty and happiness that she associates with the white, middle-class world. They also come to symbolize her own blindness, for she gains blue eyes only at the cost of her sanity. The "bluest" eye could also mean the saddest eye. Furthermore, *eye* puns on *I*, in the sense that the novel's title uses the singular form of the noun (instead of *The Bluest Eyes*) to express many of the characters' sad isolation.

THE MARIGOLDS

Claudia and Frieda associate marigolds with the safety and well-being of Pecola's baby. Their ceremonial offering of money and the remaining unsold marigold seeds represents an honest sacrifice on their part. They believe that if the marigolds they have planted grow, then Pecola's baby will be all right. More generally, marigolds represent the constant renewal of nature. In Pecola's case, this cycle of renewal is perverted by her father's rape of her.

SUMMARY & ANALYSIS

PROLOGUE

SUMMARY: PART ONE

> *We had dropped our seeds in our own little plot of*
> *black dirt just as Pecola's father had dropped his seeds*
> *in his own plot of black dirt.* (See QUOTATIONS, p. 51)

The novel begins with a series of sentences that seem to come from a children's reader. The sentences describe a house and the family that lives in the house—Mother, Father, Dick, and Jane. The brief narrative focuses on Jane. The pet cat will not play with Jane, and when Jane asks her mother to play, she laughs. When Jane asks her father to play, he smiles, and the dog runs away instead of playing with Jane. Then a friend comes to play with Jane. This sequence is repeated verbatim without punctuation, and then is repeated a third time without spaces between the words or punctuation.

SUMMARY: PART TWO

An unnamed narrator explains that there were no marigolds in the fall of 1941, when she was nine years old. She relates that she and her sister believed that there were no marigolds because Pecola, a slightly older black girl, was having her father's baby; it was not only their own marigold seeds that did not sprout—none of the marigolds in the community did. The sisters believed that if they said the right words over the seeds, the seeds would blossom and Pecola's baby would be safely delivered. But the seeds refused to sprout, and the two sisters blamed each other for this failure in order to relieve their sense of guilt. For years, the narrator believed that her sister was right—that she had planted the seeds too deeply. But now she believes the earth itself was barren and that their hope was no more productive than Pecola's father's despair. The narrator states that the sisters' innocence, Pecola's baby, and Pecola's father are all dead; only Pecola and the earth remain. She concludes by indicating that it would be too difficult to explain why these events happened, so she will instead relate how they happened.

ANALYSIS

Each section of this prologue gives, in a different way, an overview of the novel as a whole. At a glance, the Dick-and-Jane motif alerts us to the fact that for the most part the story will be told from a child's perspective. Just as the Dick-and-Jane primer teaches children how to read, this novel will be about the larger story of how children learn to interpret their world. But there is something wrong with the Dick-and-Jane narrative as it is presented here. Because the sentences are not spread out with pictures, as they would be in an actual reader, we become uncomfortably aware of their shortness and abruptness. The paragraph that these sentences comprise lacks cohesion; it is unclear how each individual observation builds on the last. In the same way, the children in this novel lack ways to connect the disjointed, often frightening experiences that make up their lives. The substance of the narrative, though written in resolutely cheerful language, is also disturbing. Though we are told that the family that lives in the pretty house is happy, Jane is isolated. Not only do her parents and pets refuse to play with her, but they seem to refuse any direct communication with her. When Jane approaches her mother to play, the mother simply laughs, which makes us wonder if the mother actually is, as we have been told, "very nice." When she asks her father to play, her father only smiles. The lack of connection between sentences mirrors the lack of connection between the individuals in this story.

When the Dick-and-Jane story repeats without divisions between the sentences, its individual components are more connected because they are run together more, but this kind of connection is not a meaningful one. Instead, the meaninglessness of the sequence becomes more noticeable, even shocking, because the sequence is sped up. In the third repetition, when all the words run together, the speed and closeness of the connection between the elements of the story make it nearly unreadable. This third repetition alerts us that the story that follows operates in two related ways: it presents a sequence of images that are isolated from one another, and it presents a sequence of images that are connected by sheer momentum rather than any inherent relationship. This repetition implicitly warns us to expect a story that is vivid but fragmented.

The second section of the prologue gives a more conventional overview of the story, as the narrator looks back on the events the novel will recount and tells the reader how it will end. This anticipation of the story not only creates suspense (we are immediately curious about Pecola and her father), but also, like the repetitions in the Dick-and-Jane section, gives a sense of circularity. This story cannot simply be told once and forgotten. It contains some central mysteries that its characters must return to again and again.

While the two parts of the prologue resemble one another in function, they differ in expression. Whereas the first section is marked by a lack of connection between ideas, people, and sentences, the second section is filled with such connections, including a association between the natural cycles of the earth and the unnatural components of the story—a traditional literary device that contributes to the section's lyrical feeling. Even though the narrator believes that she and her sister were foolish to think that there was some connection between their flower bed and Pecola's baby, a parallel nonetheless persists. There is an emotional connection between Pecola, her baby, and the sisters who are worried for them, and there is a cause-and-effect connection between the sisters' actions and the success of their planting. There is also a connection between action and questions of morality—the sisters feel guilty that their seeds have not grown, and they look for someone to blame. These are the kinds of connections that give a story meaning, in opposition to the seemingly meaningless order of the Dick-and-Jane sentences. Thus, Morrison's two-part prologue has set up a structure for the work as a whole, and the novel moves between the extremes of the meaningless, fractured, and damaged (represented by the first part of the prologue), and the meaningful, lyrical, and whole (represented by the second).

AUTUMN: CHAPTER 1

SUMMARY

Outside a Greek hotel, Rosemary Villanucci, a white neighbor of the MacTeer family, taunts Claudia and Frieda MacTeer from the Villanucci's Buick. School has started, and the sisters are expected to help gather coal that has fallen out of the railroad cars. Their house is spacious but old, drafty, and infested with rodents. During one trip to gather coal, Claudia catches a cold. Her mother is angry but takes good care of Claudia, who does not understand that her mother is mad at the sickness, not her. Frieda comforts Claudia by singing to her—or at least Claudia remembers it this way. In hindsight, she also remembers the constant, implicit presence of love.

The MacTeers are getting a new boarder, Henry Washington. The children overhear their mother explaining that he was living with the elderly Della Jones but that she has grown too senile for him to stay there. Mrs. MacTeer also explains that Miss Jones's husband ran off with another woman because he thought his wife smelled too clean. Henry has never married and has the reputation of being a steady worker. Mrs. MacTeer says the extra money will help her. When Henry arrives, the children adore him because he teases them and then does a magic trick: he offers them a penny but then makes it disappear so that the girls must find it hidden on his person.

There is also a second addition to the MacTeer household, Pecola Breedlove. She is temporarily in county custody because her father burned down the family's house. Pecola is the object of pity because her father has put the family "outdoors," one of the greatest sins by community standards. Having joined the MacTeers, Pecola loves drinking milk out of their Shirley Temple cup. Claudia explains that she has always hated Shirley Temple and also the blonde, blue-eyed baby doll that she was given for Christmas. She is confused about why everyone else thinks such dolls are lovable, and she pulls apart her doll trying to discover where its "beauty" is located. Taking apart the doll to the core, she discovers only a "mere metal roundness." The adults are outraged, but Claudia points out that they never asked her what she wanted for Christmas. She explains that her hatred of dolls turned into a hatred of little white girls and then into a false love of whiteness and cleanliness.

It is a Saturday afternoon, and Mrs. MacTeer is angry because Pecola has drunk three quarts of milk. The girls are avoiding Mrs. MacTeer and sitting bored on the steps when Pecola begins bleeding from between her legs. Frieda understands that Pecola is menstruating (though she calls it "ministratin'") and attempts to attach a pad to Pecola's dress. Meanwhile, Rosemary, who has been watching from the bushes, yells to Mrs. MacTeer that the girls are "playing nasty." Mrs. MacTeer starts to whip Frieda, but then sees the pad, and the girls explain what has happened. Mrs. MacTeer is sorry and cleans up Pecola. That night in bed, Pecola asks Frieda how babies are made. Frieda says you have to get someone to love you. Pecola asks, "How do you get someone to love you?"

ANALYSIS

This chapter introduces the various forms of powerlessness that Claudia faces and the challenges that she will encounter as she grows up. First of all, she experiences the universal powerlessness of being a child. Raised in an era when children are to be seen, not heard, she and her sister view adults as unpredictable forces that must be watched and handled carefully. Next, Claudia experiences the powerlessness of being black and poor in the 1940s. She and her family cling to the margins of society, with the dangerous threat of homelessness looming. Finally, Claudia experiences the powerlessness of being female in a world in which the position of women is precarious. Indeed, being a child, being black, and being a girl are conditions of powerlessness that reinforce one another so much that for Claudia they become impossible to separate.

Though Claudia is careful to point out that fear of poverty and homelessness was a more prevalent day-to-day worry in her community than fear of discrimination, racism does affect her life in subtle yet profound ways, especially in the sense that it distorts her beauty standards. Morrison most notably uses the cultural icon of Shirley Temple (a hugely popular child actress of the day) and the popular children's dolls of the 1940s to illustrate mass culture's influence on young black girls. When Claudia states that, unlike Frieda, she has not reached the point in her psychological "development" when her hatred of Shirley Temple and dolls will turn to love, the irony of the statement is clear. Claudia naïvely assumes that the beauty others see in the doll must inhere physically *inside* it, and so she takes apart the doll to search for its beauty. She has not yet learned that beauty is a matter of cultural norms and that the doll is beautiful not in and of itself but rather because the culture she lives in believes whiteness is superior.

Claudia's hatred of white dolls extends to white girls, and Morrison uses this process as a starting point to study the complex love-hate relationship between blacks and whites. What horrifies Claudia most about her own treatment of white girls is the disinterested nature of her hatred. Claudia hates them for their whiteness, not for more defensible personal reasons. Ultimately, her shame of her own hatred hides itself in pretended love. By describing the sequence of hating whiteness but then coming to embrace it, Claudia diagnoses the black community's worship of white images (as well as cleanliness and denial of the body's desires) as a complicated kind of self-hatred. It is not simply that black people learn to believe that whiteness is beautiful because they are surrounded by white America's advertisements and movies; Claudia suggests that black children start with a healthy hatred of the claims to white superiority but that their guilt at their own anger then transforms hatred into a false love to compensate for that hatred.

Unlike Claudia, Pecola does not undergo a process of first rejecting then accepting America's white beauty standards. Pecola adores Shirley Temple and loves playing with dolls. Her excessive and expensive milk-drinking from the Shirley Temple is part of her desire to internalize the values of white culture—a symbolic moment that foreshadows her desire to possess blue eyes. While these desires illustrate that Pecola mentally and emotionally remains a child, her menstruation shows that she is experiencing a physical coming-of-age. Claudia and Frieda envy Pecola's menstruation, but implicit in this scene is the threat that Pecola can now become pregnant, an adult reality that turns out to be quite troubling.

The pressures that Claudia faces as a girl becoming a woman are perhaps subtler than the pressures of race, but in some ways, more prevalent. There are continual references to the fate of women done wrong by men: Della Jones is thought to be senile in part because her husband left her; Pecola is homeless because her father has beaten his wife and burned down their home; Mrs. MacTeer sings blues songs about men leaving their women; and the onset of Pecola's first period is cause for fear, confusion, and accusations of "nastiness" before becoming cause for muted celebration. The chapter ends with speculation about the connection between men, love, and babies. For Claudia, issues of racism, poverty, and standards of beauty are intimately connected to her inevitable entrance into womanhood. The same is true for Pecola, though her eventual initiation into the world of men, love, and babies is much too soon and much too violent.

AUTUMN: CHAPTER 2

SUMMARY

This short chapter is dedicated to describing the apartment, which was formerly a store, that the Breedloves move into once Cholly Breedlove, Pecola's father, is out of jail. Nowadays the storefront is abandoned, and so the narrator moves backward in time. Before it was abandoned, the storefront housed a pizza parlor, and before that, a Hungarian bakery, and before that, a Gypsy family. The narrator supposes that no one remembers the time when the Breedloves lived there, back when the storefront was divided into two rooms by some wooden planks. In the front room, there are two sofas, a piano, and an artificial Christmas tree that has not been taken down for two years. In the bedroom are beds for Pecola, her brother, Sammy, and their parents, and a temperamental coal stove. The kitchen is in a separate room in the back.

The narrator focuses on the furnishings. The furniture is aged but not by frequent use; it does not hold any memories. It has been "conceived, manufactured, shipped, and sold in various states of thoughtlessness, greed, and indifference." The only piece of furniture that calls up any emotion is the couch, which fills its owner with anger. Though bought new, the couch has a split down the middle, and the store refuses to take it back. The coal stove seems to have a mind of its own; its heat is unpredictable. One thing is certain: the fire will always be dead in the morning.

ANALYSIS

This chapter, which focuses solely on describing the Breedlove apartment, reads like a playwright's instructions for a set. Morrison produces a great deal of meaning from small details. Almost every object in the scene can be interpreted symbolically. The ugliness of the abandoned storefront and its refusal to blend in with the other buildings that surround it symbolize the ugliness of the Breedloves' story—a story not only about the ugliness they create but also about the ugliness perpetrated against them. Just as the storefront has now been abandoned, they have been abandoned by one another and by the world around them. This sad isolation is somewhat lightened by the description of the other inhabitants of the storefront: the teenage boys who hang out in front of the pizza parlor are filled with a youthful restlessness more attractive than menacing, and their inexperience at smoking expresses their vulnerability. The Hungarian bakery conjures up sensual satisfaction and comfort, and the description of the Gypsy family suggests that people living on the margins can sometimes look and be looked at without fear. The Gypsy girls sit in the windows, sometimes winking or beckoning to passersby, but mostly watching the world go by. This flow of everyday life reminds us that, as desperate as the Breedloves' circumstances are, is just one among many neighborhood stories.

Even though the Breedloves live in a dwelling so depressing that it borders on hyperbole, we are reminded that each member of the family still draws meaning from the home they make together. Although there is frightfully little material for the imagination to work with, Morrison suggests that human beings always invest meaning in objects, no matter how tawdry they may be. Morrison writes that each member of the Breedlove family pieces together a quilt based upon "fragments of experience" and "tiny impressions," salvaging the best of what they have. In her vision of what the Breedlove family lacks, Morrison imagines a world in which a sofa is defined by what has been lost or found in it, what comfort it has provided or what loving has been conducted upon it. A bed is defined by someone giving birth in it, a Christmas tree by the young girl who looks at it. The Breedlove home lacks these kinds of positive symbols. Just as their family name is ironic (they do the opposite of their name), the few household objects they do possess—a ripped couch, a cold stove—are symbolic of suffering and degradation rather than of home.

This chapter also makes a point that the novel continually reinforces: giving life meaning is an essential, universal, and relentless human activity. While we might understand Morrison's insistence on the symbolic meaning of the couch or stove as a mark of her gifts as a novelist, her point is that the Breedloves *themselves* understand these objects as symbolic. Each character in the novel is, in a sense, a storyteller, making order out of his or her unordered experiences, sometimes in ways that are constructive and sometimes in ways that are destructive.

AUTUMN: CHAPTER 3

> . . . [I]f those eyes of hers were different, that is to say,
> beautiful, she herself would be different.
> (See QUOTATIONS, p. 52)

SUMMARY

The narrator announces that the Breedloves live in the storefront because they are black and poor, and because they believe they are ugly. They are not objectively ugly. Though they have small, closely set eyes and heavy eyebrows, they also have high cheekbones and shapely lips. They are ugly because they believe they are ugly. The action that now unfolds takes place on a Saturday morning in October. Mrs. Breedlove wakes first and begins banging around in the kitchen. Pecola is awake in bed and knows that her mother will pick a fight with her father, who came home drunk the previous night. Each of Cholly's drunken episodes ends with a fight with his wife. Mrs. Breedlove comes in and attempts to wake Cholly to bring her some coal for the stove. He refuses, and she says that if she sneezes just once from fetching the coal outside, he is in trouble.

The narrator comments that Mrs. Breedlove and Cholly need each other—she needs him to reinforce her identity as a martyr and to give shape to an otherwise dreary life, and he needs to take out a lifetime of hurt upon her. When Cholly was young, two white men once caught having sex with a girl. They forced him to continue while they watched. Instead of hating the white men, Cholly hated the girl. Because of this and other humiliations, Cholly is a violent and cruel man. The fights between him and Mrs. Breedlove follow a predictable pattern, and the two have an unstated agreement not to kill each other. Sammy usually either runs away from home or joins the fight. Pecola tries to find ways to endure the pain.

Predictably, Mrs. Breedlove sneezes, and the fight begins. She douses Cholly with cold water and he begins to beat her. She hits him with the dishpan and then a stove lid. Sammy helps by hitting his father on the head. Once Cholly is knocked out, Sammy urges his mother to kill him, and she quiets him. Pecola, still in bed, feels nauseated. As she often does, she wills herself to disappear. She can imagine each body part dissolving except for her eyes. She hates her ugliness, which makes teachers and classmates ignore her. For a long time, she has hoped and prayed for blue eyes, which will make her beautiful and change all the evil in her life to good.

Pecola walks to the grocery store to buy candy. She wonders why people consider dandelions ugly. She decides to buy Mary Janes, but she has difficulty communicating with Mr. Yacobowski, the store owner, who seems to look right through her. He does not understand what she is pointing at and speaks harshly to her. He does not want to touch her hand when she passes over her money. Walking home, Pecola is angry but most of all ashamed. She decides dandelions are ugly, whereas blonde, blue-eyed Mary Jane, pictured on the candy wrapper, is beautiful.

Pecola goes to visit the whores who live in the apartment above hers, China, Poland, and Miss Marie. They are good-natured and affectionate with her, and they tell her about their "boyfriends" (Pecola's term for their clients). Miss Marie tells stories about turning one of her boyfriends over to the FBI and about Dewey Prince, the one man she truly loved. The narrator tells us that these are not hookers with hearts of gold or women whose innocence has been betrayed. Quite simply, these women cheerfully and unsentimentally hate men. They feel neither ashamed of nor victimized by their profession. Pecola wonders what love is like. She wonders if it is like her parents' lovemaking, during which her father sounds as if he is in pain and her mother is dead silent.

ANALYSIS

This chapter portrays victimhood as a complex phenomenon rather than a simple, direct relationship between oppressor and oppressed. The Breedloves' ugliness is one of the central mysteries of the novel. It cannot be attributed to their literal appearance (we are told that their ugliness "did not belong to them"), nor simply to the cultural images that indicate that only whiteness is beautiful. Instead, the narrator suggests, it seems

> as though some mysterious all-knowing master had said, 'You are ugly people.' . . . [a]nd they took the ugliness in their hands, threw it as a mantle over them, and went about the world with it.

While the use of the word "master" suggests a connection to the history of slavery, the Breedloves' ugliness has been both foisted on them and chosen, an identity that is destructive but that still gives a sense of meaning to their existence. Mrs. Breedlove's sense of martyrdom is similar. While it is clear that in some sense she consents to, and even chooses, the abuse she takes from her husband, it is also clear that this abuse damages her. The violence gives her life meaning, gives her days dramatic shape, and gives her the opportunity to exercise her imagination, but it is clear that these things are deeply wrong. The meaning she finds is senseless violence, the dramatic shape is tragic, and this exercise of her imagination is self-destructive. It appears that the will to make meaning out of one's life can be a negative power as well as a positive one, especially if one's life has been damaged by mistreatment.

This chapter also introduces the symbolic story that Pecola fantasizes for her own life. She decides that if she had beautiful blue eyes, her life would magically right itself. She wants blue eyes for two reasons—so that she can change what she sees, and so that she can change how others see her. For Pecola, these reasons are interchangeable because she believes that how people see her (as ugly) creates what she sees (hurtful behavior). While her brother has the option of running away from these terrible domestic scenes, Pecola, a young girl with fewer choices, believes she can change what she sees only by changing herself. There are moments when she temporarily succeeds in breaking the destructive connection between what she sees and how people see her. When she considers that dandelions might be beautiful, she implicitly recognizes that beauty can be created by seeing rather than by being seen. By the same logic, she could redefine herself as beautiful even without blue eyes. But her humiliation at the grocer's store reinforces the old idea that ugliness is inherent and cannot be changed by a different way of perceiving the world. When the grocer looks at her with a blankness tinged with distaste, she does not consider that he is ugly—she only considers herself to be so. After she leaves the grocery store, she briefly experiences a healthy anger, but it gives way to shame. Pecola interprets poor treatment and abuse as her own fault. She believes that the way people observe her is more real than what she herself observes.

WINTER: CHAPTER 4

SUMMARY

Winter arrives, which means boredom and the long wait for spring. But this winter, the arrival of a new girl named Maureen Peal breaks the monotony. She is a light-skinned, wealthy black girl who enchants the whole school. Claudia and Frieda dislike her and search for flaws. They are relieved to discover that she has a dog tooth and stumps where her sixth fingers were removed. She has a locker next to Claudia's, and one day she suggests that she walk part way home with Claudia and Frieda.

Soon the three girls come upon a circle of boys harassing Pecola. Shouting a derogatory chant, they taunt her for her black skin and because her father sleeps naked. Frieda comes to the rescue, hitting one boy and threatening another. Claudia joins the fray, and it looks as if the boys will beat up the MacTeer girls, but then Maureen arrives on the scene. The boys do not want to fight in front of Maureen and leave. Maureen takes Pecola's arm and talks to her about movies and gym class. She asks the girls if they want some ice cream and treats Pecola. Claudia is embarrassed because she thought Maureen would treat her as well. Instead, she goes without ice cream. The girls talk about menstruation, and Maureen asks Pecola if she has ever seen a naked man. Pecola says she has never seen her father naked, and Maureen presses the issue. Claudia and Frieda tell Maureen to cut it out, and Claudia remembers the shame and strange interest of seeing her own father naked. The girls argue: Claudia accuses Maureen of being boy-crazy, and Maureen tells the girls they are black and ugly. Pecola is pained, and Claudia secretly worries that what Maureen has said is true.

When the girls arrive home, only Henry is there. He gives them money for ice cream, but they decide to buy candy instead because they do not want to run into Maureen again. When they come home, they see Henry entertaining the prostitutes China and the Maginot Line (Miss Marie) in the living room. Claudia and Frieda are disturbed because they know that their mother hates these women. The girls come in after the women leave, and Frieda asks Henry about them. He lies and says they are members of his Bible-study group. The girls decide to keep his secret.

ANALYSIS

The introduction of the light-skinned black girl Maureen reinforces the novel's earlier message of the Shirley Temple cup—whiteness is beautiful and blackness is ugly. Maureen also reinforces the connection between race and class—lighter-skinned than the other black children, she is also wealthier. At first, Claudia responds to Maureen with jealousy—she simply wants the pretty things Maureen has. But this jealousy gives way to a more destructive envy, as Claudia begins to suspect that in order to have the things that Maureen has, she must look like Maureen. She remains puzzled, however, by what Maureen has and what she lacks. She explains that, at this point, she and her sister were still in love with themselves and enjoyed their own bodies. They had not yet learned self-hatred. But Maureen is the harbinger of the self-hatred that will come with the onset of womanhood, when physical beauty becomes more important and the body becomes easier to shame. Claudia is perceptive enough to understand at this point that it is not Maureen she hates and fears, but whatever it is that makes Maureen cute and the MacTeer girls ugly.

As with the Shirley Temple cup in the first chapter, the use of popular culture in this chapter provides commentary on the mass media's preference for whiteness—and the effect this preference has on the lives of young girls. In a revealing moment, Maureen recounts the plot of a movie she has seen in which the light-skinned daughter of a white man rejects her black mother but then cries at her mother's funeral. It is clear that Maureen revels in the melodramatic, without recognizing that it may be a reflection of her own assumption of superiority and perhaps her own relationship with her mother (who has seen the movie four times). Racist messages are so prevalent that they are difficult to see. They are as commonplace as drinking milk from a cup or enjoying a movie.

This chapter also gives a brief portrait of the cultural pressures that black boys experience. We are told that their meanness to Pecola is an expression of their own self-hatred. They can taunt her for being black—"Black e mo Black e mo"—because they hate their own blackness. This self-hatred, along with their "cultivated ignorance" and "designed hopelessness," is, like Pecola's ugliness, a state of being that is both forced upon them and chosen. At this point, the boys are still vulnerable. Claudia and Frieda can stop them in their tracks, and Frieda threatens to reveal that one of the boys still wets his bed. But we can anticipate that the children's even playing field will not last when the boys become men and the girls become women. All the players in this scene are experiencing their last moments of childhood before sex changes everything.

The mystery and fear of sex hangs over this chapter. Maureen introduces the subjects of menstruation, babies, and naked men, and though Claudia and Frieda try to silence her, their fear reveals that this topic has a power over them too. Claudia remembers her father's nakedness as both disturbing and oddly "friendly," and Pecola's defensiveness about her own father's nakedness foreshadows the sexual intimacy he forces upon her later in the novel. When Claudia sees Henry entertaining the prostitutes, even though she does not understand what is happening, she feels "terror and obscure longing." There is a hint that sex makes adults behave like something other than responsible caregivers. Sex will disrupt the order that, even though it sometimes galls Claudia, gives her a sense of stability and comfort.

WINTER: CHAPTER 5

SUMMARY

This chapter describes in detail a particular type of black woman. She comes from some small, rural town in the South, full of natural beauty, where everyone has a job. She takes special care of her body and her clothes. She goes to a land-grant college and learns how to do the work reserved for her, the care and feeding of white people, with grace and good manners. She marries and bears the children of a man who knows that she will take good care of his house and his clothes. But she also is a tyrant over her home and over her own body. She does not enjoy sex. She feels affection only for the household cat, which is as neat and quiet as she is. She caresses and cuddles the cat in a way that she refuses to caress or cuddle her family.

Then such a woman enters the novel. Her name is Geraldine, she is married to a man named Louis, and they have a son named Junior. Geraldine takes excellent physical care of Junior, but early on, he understands that she feels real affection only for the cat. In response, he tortures the cat and torments children who come to play at the nearby school playground. Junior would have liked to have played with the black children, but his mother will let him play only with upper-class "colored" people, not lower-class "niggers."

One day, a bored and isolated Junior decides to pick on Pecola, who is passing through the playground. She tells him she does not want to play, but he lures her into his home by promising to show her some kittens. Pecola is overwhelmed by the beauty and cleanliness of the house. Meanwhile, Junior throws the family cat, which has black fur and blue eyes, in her face. Scratched and shaken, Pecola tries to leave, but Junior stands on the other side of the door and shuts her in. The cat begins to rub against Pecola, and its friendliness distracts her from crying. She caresses the cat as Junior opens the door. Angered that the cat is getting attention, he picks it up and swings it around by one of its hind legs. The cat is terrified, and Pecola tries to rescue it. When she pulls Junior down, he lets go of the cat, and it hits the radiator and collapses in a lifeless heap. At this moment, Geraldine comes home, and Junior tells her that Pecola has killed the cat. Geraldine calls Pecola a "nasty little black bitch" and sends her away.

ANALYSIS

From what we have seen of the squalor of Pecola's home life, we might imagine that a more orderly life in a middle-class home would give her a happier existence. But in this chapter, it becomes clear that material comfort, neatness, and quiet can become deadly themselves if not accompanied by genuine human warmth. The chapter opens with a deceptively positive description of the kind of woman that we will learn to hate by the chapter's close. Her hometown has a beautiful name, and her girlhood involves a close relationship to the beauties of nature. She is soft and sweet, not shrill and hard like some of her urban sisters. She smells good and sings in church. But all these details exist only to drive home the point that such surface traits say little about a person's inner goodness, and, in fact, can be misleading.

The narrator suggests that this emphasis on propriety and cleanliness actually functions as a deep form of self-betrayal. These women are educated but seem so only to be more submissive to white men. They are trained, above all, "to get rid of the funkiness"—the disorderliness of human passion and personality. Though they take good care of their husbands' clothes and feed them well, they do these chores out of a sense of propriety, not a feeling of love. Their well-kept homes must be defended against human dirt and mess. They have experienced sexual pleasure by accident on their own but seem incapable of taking pleasure in their husbands' bodies. They expect their children to be as emotionally repressed as they are.

Geraldine's emphasis on decorum and cleanliness also represents Morrison's critique of a particular kind of internalized racism and a middle-class contempt for the poor. Throughout the book, the worship of whiteness has been associated with the worship of cleanliness, and the MacTeer girls' pleasure in their own dirt has been a mark of their self-esteem and physical confidence. Geraldine's hatred of dirt and disorder is fundamentally linked to her hatred of "niggers" and is, of course, a kind of self-hatred. She scapegoats poor, dark-skinned black children—in this instance, Pecola—because she hates her own blackness. This scapegoating is intensified by fear: the fear that it is not so easy to distinguish between respectable "colored" people and "niggers" after all, and the fear of the suffering she sees in the eyes of black girls like Pecola.

This chapter also demonstrates how those who hate most often misdirect both their feelings of love and their feelings of hatred, multiplying the suffering of the oppressed. Geraldine, instead of directing her hatred toward the subtle racism that requires her to repress the disorderly parts of herself, expresses hatred toward her own family through her coldness. Meanwhile, she misdirects her capacity for affection toward the family pet. Junior, who hates his mother for her coldness, redirects his hatred toward the cat and Pecola. The extremity of Junior's sadism suggests that children suffer from emotional neglect and misplaced hatred in particularly intense ways. Pecola and the cat (which, it is important to note, resembles Pecola in its blackness and possesses the blue eyes she desires) then become Junior's scapegoats, suffering the effects of a hatred that has nothing to do with them. Pecola's father will repeat this pattern when he takes out his hatred of everyone who has hurt him upon his daughter.

SPRING: CHAPTER 6

SUMMARY

Spring arrives, and Claudia associates this event with being whipped with a switch instead of a strap. She lies in an empty lot ruminating and then heads home. She finds her mother singing and behaving strangely, absentmindedly doing the same chore twice. She finds Frieda upstairs crying. It turns out that Henry touched Frieda's breasts. Frieda ran from the house to find her parents, who were in the garden, and told them what had happened. She returned with her parents to the house, but Henry was gone. When he returned, Mr. and Mrs. MacTeer attacked him. A neighbor, Mr. Buford, arrived and gave Mr. MacTeer a gun. He shot at Henry and Henry ran away. Rosemary Villanucci came out and told Frieda that her father would go to jail, and Frieda hit her. Then another neighbor, Miss Dunion, came in and suggested that they take Frieda to the doctor because she might be "ruined," a fear that now makes Frieda weep.

Frieda and Claudia are confused about what "ruined" means and worry that Frieda will become fat like the Maginot Line. They understand that China and Poland are "ruined" as well but think that they are not fat because they drink whiskey. Frieda and Claudia decide to ask Pecola to get whisky from her father in order to keep Frieda from getting fat. They go to Pecola's house, but no one is home. The Maginot Line is upstairs on the porch drinking root beer, and she tells the children that Pecola is helping her mother at her workplace. She invites the girls upstairs for a soda, but Frieda tells her that they are not allowed to visit her because she is "ruined."

The Maginot Line throws the root-beer bottle at the girls in anger, but then she laughs. Claudia and Frieda run away and decide that even though Pecola's mother works on the other side of town, Frieda's situation is dire enough that they should go find her.

Frieda and Claudia walk to the lakefront houses, in a beautiful neighborhood with a park that is for white children only. They find Pecola at the back of one of the prettiest houses. She is surprised to see them, and they ask her why she is not afraid of the Maginot Line. Pecola is confused and talks about how nice Miss Marie (that is, the Maginot Line) and her friends are. Mrs. Breedlove sticks her head out the door, is introduced to the girls, and tells them they can wait with Pecola for the laundry and then walk back to town with her. The inside of the house is beautiful, and a small white girl comes in and asks for "Polly." Claudia is furious that the child calls Mrs. Breedlove by this name because even Pecola calls her mother "Mrs. Breedlove." From upstairs, the little girl calls for Polly, and Pecola accidentally pulls a freshly baked berry cobbler off the counter. The cobbler splatters on the floor and burns her, and her mother comes in and beats her. Furious, Mrs. Breedlove sends the girls away and comforts the little white girl, who has begun to cry.

ANALYSIS
This chapter emphasizes the ignorance and confusion that accompany Frieda's experience of becoming a sexual being. Frieda is not given the chance to step gradually into her sexual identity; instead, this identity is forced upon her by an adult. Frieda is uncertain how to describe what has happened to her. She knows that Henry's actions are inappropriate, but she does not understand what they mean. Claudia wonders, almost enviously, how being touched in this way feels, but Frieda rejects this question—what is important is not how she feels but what has been done to her and how her parents react. She depends upon their interpretation of what has taken place in order to understand it herself. But they still do not know what "ruined" means, and not understanding what makes the prostitute distasteful to their mother, they focus on what makes the prostitute distasteful to them—her fatness. The Maginot Line's nickname comes from the bulky defensive fortifications built before World War II to protect the border of France from Germany. The thinness of her companions is then connected to whisky (again based on something that they have heard their mother say, but

which they misunderstood), and so they undertake a quest to procure whisky for Frieda. In a sense, the way the MacTeer girls read and misread the adult world echoes the Dick-and-Jane reader at the beginning of the novel.

This logical but mistaken chain of reasoning adds a rare note of humor to the story that is unfolding. Frieda's experience is frightening and confusing, but she is quickly defended by her protective parents, and Henry is a foolish rather than a threatening figure. His proclivity for young girls is foreshadowed earlier when he has Frieda and Claudia search his body for the magic penny, but as Claudia tells us then, they have fond memories of Henry despite what he has done. Frieda is angered by her experience and ready to take action rather than remain ashamed and defeated. Her experience of unwanted sexual attention contrasts sharply with Pecola's rape experience, in which Pecola's father not only fails to protect her, but is the perpetrator himself.

The messages the girls hear about white superiority do not come only from the white media or light-skinned blacks like Geraldine. More scarring and memorable than any prior source in the novel, Pecola's own mother reinforces the message the girls have been receiving about the superiority of whites. The white neighborhood in which Mrs. Breedlove works is beautiful and well kept, demonstrating the connection between race and class. The kitchen is spotless, with white porcelain and white woodwork. The little white girl is dressed in delicate pink and has yellow hair. In contrast, Pecola spills "blackish blueberries" all over the floor, underlining the connection between blackness and mess. Her mother reinforces this connection as well. Instead of worrying that her own daughter has been burned by the hot berries, she pushes Pecola down into the pie juice. She then comforts the little white girl and begins to clean the black stain off of her pink dress. When she speaks to Pecola and her friends, her voice is like "rotten pieces of apple," but when she speaks to the white girl, her voice is like honey. Her desire to disavow her daughter is proved when the white girl asks who the black children were and Mrs. Breedlove avoids answering her. She has renounced her own black family for the family of her white employer.

SPRING: CHAPTER 7

SUMMARY

This chapter recounts Mrs. Breedlove's story. She grows up in Alabama as Pauline Williams, and when she is two years old, she impales her foot on a nail. Forever afterward, she walks with a slight limp, and she believes that this accident determined her destiny. During her childhood, she is isolated from other family members, and therefore cultivates her own pleasures. She enjoys arranging things, creating order and neatness out of clutter. Her family later migrates to Kentucky, where they move into a sizable house with a garden. Pauline is put in charge of caring for the house and her two younger siblings, Chicken and Pie. She enjoys this life, but once she turns fifteen, she becomes restless and melancholy. She begins to dream of a stranger—a man, or a god—who will take her away with him.

Then one day, a stranger arrives. Pauline is standing in the garden and hears a young man whistling. Suddenly she feels him tickling her bad foot and turns to meet the gaze of Cholly Breedlove. They fall in love, and he treats her with tenderness. They decide to marry and move up north to Lorain, Ohio, where there are more jobs. Then life becomes more difficult. Pauline feels lonely and isolated, and she is surprised by how unfriendly the other women are. They are amused by her country ways. She begins to long for clothes that will make the women look at her differently, and she and Cholly begin to argue about money. Cholly's drinking becomes a problem.

At this point, Pauline takes her first job as a housekeeper in a white woman's house. The white woman is well-off but petty and foolish. Her family has dirty habits. One day, Cholly shows up at the woman's house drunk and demands money, and Pauline leaves her job. The woman will not give her the job back or the rest of her pay unless Pauline leaves Cholly. Pauline refuses and is left without money for cooking gas.

Soon thereafter Pauline realizes she is pregnant. Cholly is happy and their marriage improves, but Pauline is still lonely in their apartment. She takes refuge in the movies and develops destructive ideas about physical beauty and romantic love. She tries to make herself look like a movie star, but then while chewing candy at a movie, she loses one of her front teeth. From then on, she feels ugly, and she and

Cholly begin to fight again. Her first baby fails to fill the hole in her life. She talks to her second baby in the womb, vowing to love her no matter what. When she gives birth in the hospital, a doctor tells a group of students that black women do not feel pain while giving birth; they are "just like horses." Despite this insult, Pauline is pleased with her new baby, Pecola, but knows the baby is ugly.

Pauline then takes on her identity as martyr. She joins the church and becomes the family breadwinner, securing a job with the Fishers, a wealthy family who appreciate her good work. She loves her work because it allows her to make things beautiful and orderly. She begins to neglect her own house and family. At times, she remembers the good times with Cholly, when their lovemaking turned everything into rainbows. Now their lovemaking occurs while he is drunk and she is half-asleep.

ANALYSIS

Morrison uses the technique of shifting perspectives to allow us different ways of judging characters. In this chapter, we are given a new take on the story that is unfolding, the perspective of Pecola's mother. In the previous chapter, she behaved terribly toward her daughter, and we are ready to condemn her. But now we learn why she behaves the way she does, and our perception of what took place becomes complicated by her past. Like every other character in the book, Pauline is partly a victim of circumstances and has partly chosen her own fate. Though we may condemn some of her choices, we now sympathize with the experiences that have made these choices seem necessary.

Stylistically, Pauline's story is told in the most sympathetic terms. The majority of it is told by an omniscient narrator, with the more poignant moments of her story narrated by Pauline herself and set off in italics. Our sympathy for Pauline comes in part because of the difficult circumstances she has faced—a deformed foot, loneliness, poverty, racism, and an alternately cruel and tender husband. The sections she narrates herself deal with even more personal subjects: her love for Cholly, her experience of pregnancy, and the mistreatment she receives from others. As well as mixing third-person and first-person narration, Morrison uses color to emphasize the beauty of Pauline and Cholly's relationship. Pauline describes the green flash of the june bugs that she misses from her hometown. When she falls in love with Cholly, this green imagery merges with a memory of having her hips stained purple while picking berries and the yellow of her mother's lemonade. When she remembers her and Cholly's lovemaking, these colors reappear and form a rainbow. This repetition gives a lyricism to Pauline's memories.

Like the other characters in the novel, Pauline creates narratives to explain her life. These stories provide her life with meaning, but the meanings she creates are frequently damaging. She imagines that she is isolated because of her deformed foot, and accepts this isolation as her fate, when in fact she might have countered her isolation by being more outgoing. She falls in love with Cholly in part because he fits the story she has been telling herself about the stranger who will come to her. Without this story, she might have noticed sooner that they are not perfect for each other. Her addiction to the movies is most damaging in this regard; she comes to believe the stories that imply that love is about beauty and possession rather than about "lust and simple caring for." According to the narrator, romantic love and physical beauty are "[p]robably the most destructive ideas in the history of human thought." The movies Pauline sees are destructive because they are imposed from the outside rather than created from her own experiences and needs. Finally, she considers the story she tells herself about her position in the Fisher family as more meaningful than the story of her relationship to her own family, causing her daughter great suffering.

But Pauline is also able to tell stories that reinforce her rightful self-confidence and the genuine pleasure she has been able to find in her life. She clearly sees the foolishness of her first employer and the wrongs of the doctor who claims that black women feel no pain. She creates a narrative of love for Pecola before Pecola is born. Finally, she weaves the lyrical story of her love with Cholly, creating a brief oasis of beauty and joy in the midst of bleakness.

SPRING: CHAPTER 8

SUMMARY
This chapter recounts the history of Cholly Breedlove. His mother abandons him on a trash heap when he is four days old, but his Great Aunt Jimmy rescues him. She beats his mother and his mother runs away. After four years of school, Cholly gathers the courage to ask Aunt Jimmy his father's name; it is Samson Fuller. After two more years of school, Cholly takes a job at Tyson's Feed and Grain

Store and meets a man named Blue Jack. Blue Jack enthralls Cholly with his stories and shares the heart of a watermelon with him at a church picnic. Cholly remembers this kindness for a long time.

Then Aunt Jimmy gets sick. The community calls in M'Dear, the local healing woman, whose height and authority impress Cholly. She prescribes pot liquor, and Aunt Jimmy begins to improve, but then she eats a peach cobbler and dies. Cholly finds her the next morning. He does not immediately feel grief, because everyone takes care of him during the funeral and he is fascinated by all the excitement. Aunt Jimmy's brother, O.V., and his family plan to take care of him.

Cholly tries to impress one of his older cousins, Jake, by taking him to a place where the girls are. Jake persuades a girl named Suky to take a walk with him, and Cholly persuades the girl he likes, Darlene, to come along as well. They eat muscadine berries and chase each other, and then lie down to rest. When they get up to head back, Darlene tickles Cholly, and the two of them begin to touch each other. Just as Cholly is having sex for the first time, two white hunters shine their flashlights upon him. They tell him to continue while they watch, and Cholly pretends to finish. The men leave when they hear their dogs. Cholly is furious with Darlene instead of with the white men because some part of him knows that if he feels anger against the white men, it will destroy him.

It occurs to Cholly, irrationally, that Darlene might be pregnant, and he decides to run away and look for his father. He finds some money that Aunt Jimmy had hidden and spends several months working his way toward Macon, Georgia, where his father lives. He finally purchases a bus ticket, arrives in Macon, and is sent to an alley to look for his father. There he finds men gambling in various states of excitement and desperation. When he asks for Samson Fuller, he finds a man who looks especially fierce, but who is, to Cholly's surprise, shorter than he is. Samson thinks that Cholly has been sent by a creditor (or perhaps the mother of another child he has fathered) and curses him. Cholly stumbles back into the street and, in his effort not to cry, defecates in his pants. He runs to the river, hides under the pier, and washes his clothes after dark. For the first time, he feels grief for Aunt Jimmy.

From this point forward, Cholly is free in a dangerous way. He loves and beats women, he takes and leaves jobs, and he kills three white men—all the while remaining indifferent. He is indifferent about when or how he dies. He meets Pauline, and her sweetness and innocence make him want to marry her, but marriage makes him feel trapped. His interest in life is sapped, and he begins to drink. Most of all, he does not know how to relate to his children.

Now, in the present, Cholly comes home drunk and finds Pecola doing the dishes. With mixed motives of tenderness and rage, both fueled by guilt, he rapes her. She faints, and he covers her with a quilt. She wakes to find her mother looking down at her.

ANALYSIS

The novel's prologue warns us that Cholly will do something unthinkable—impregnate his own eleven-year-old daughter. If this event were told from Claudia's or Pecola's point of view, it would likely remain a senseless act of violence, something impossible to understand. But Morrison chooses to explain the rape from Cholly's point of view. Understanding how it was possible for Cholly to commit incest does not change our knowledge that he has caused tremendous suffering to his daughter but does change the nature of our horror. Cholly's violence is not frightening because it is senseless; it is frightening because it makes all too much sense, given the kind of life he has lived. Knowing Cholly's story may not change the horror of what he does, but it does make his action more bearable to us.

As with Pauline's story in the previous chapter, we sympathize with Cholly not only because he has suffered abandonment, sexual humiliation, and racism, but because there was once real beauty and joy in his life. We are given a long celebratory description about the breaking and eating of the watermelon, as if it were "[t]he nasty-sweet guts of the earth." Cholly's childlike joy in sharing the heart of the watermelon with Blue Jack is vividly rendered. Also, the pleasure of Cholly's flirtation with Darlene is narrated at length. Their bodies are compared to those of the muscadine berries. The comparison suggests that both are new and tight, not yet ripe enough to yield full pleasure, but as exciting in their promise as their full ripeness would be. The staining of Darlene's dress with berry juice recalls Pauline's memory of a similar, joyful stain. Rather than dirtiness that must be scrubbed away, here a stain is cause for celebration. In the innocence of their coming-of-age, Cholly is shy and naïve, and he tenderly helps Darlene tie her ribbon in her hair. It is she who makes the first overture, and their touching is presented as fully consensual and completely natural.

When their experience is brutally interrupted by the white men, it is clear that white power deforms black lives, rather than some kind of inherent black "dirt" that must be cleaned (as Geraldine, for example, seems to believe).

This chapter demonstrates Morrison's ability to move seamlessly between compelling, individual characters and a more generalized portrait of black life. Aunt Jimmy is an individual but is also a representative of elderly black women. She has suffered racism and abuse at the hands of her man, but she has also felt the joy of sexual love and motherhood; she has suffered violence and committed violence. Now that she is old, she is at last free—free to feel what she feels and go where she wants to go without fear.

At first glance, Aunt Jimmy's freedom seems similar to the dangerous freedom that Cholly finds, which is marked by an indifference that makes him fearless. But the novel makes a distinction: the black women understand the difference between grinding work and making love, and "the difference was all the difference there was." Cholly's depression comes when his indifference becomes a total lack of interest in life, when freedom becomes a premature desire for oblivion.

SPRING: CHAPTER 9

SUMMARY

The narrator tells the history of Soaphead Church, a self-declared "Reader, Adviser, and Interpreter of Dreams" in Lorain's black community. A light-skinned West Indian, he was raised in a family proud of its mixed blood. His family has always been academically and politically ambitious, and always corrupt. Family members have always tried to marry other light-skinned people, and, if unable to do so, they have married one another. Soaphead Church's father was a sadistic schoolmaster and his half-Chinese mother died soon after he was born. Born Elihue Micah Whitcomb, Soaphead Church soon learned the art of self-deception and developed a fascination and revulsion for dirt and decay.

Soaphead married a woman named Velma, but she left him two months afterward. Next, he pursued the ministry but soon discovered that the profession was not right for him. He studied psychiatry and other social sciences, took different jobs, and finally came to Lorain. He rents a back room from an elderly lady named Bertha

Reese, and his only hardship is her old dog, Bob, which disgusts him with its runny eyes. Soaphead buys poison to kill the dog but is too repulsed to go near it.

At this point, Pecola comes to ask him to give her blue eyes. He is touched by this request—his own attraction to whiteness makes it easily comprehensible. He knows he cannot help her, but he tells her to give meat—which he has secretly poisoned—to the dog. He tells her that if the dog reacts, her wish will be granted. The dog convulses and dies, and Pecola runs away.

Soaphead then writes a rambling and incoherent letter to God in which we learn more about his understanding of his life. He still feels rejected by Velma, who left him "the way people leave a hotel room." He describes his love for the newly budding breasts of young girls (we have already been told that he is a pedophile). He remembers two girls, Doreen and Sugar Babe, who let him touch them in exchange for money and sweets. He tells God that he did not touch Pecola and brags that he has rivaled God by granting her wish—she will not literally have blue eyes, but she will believe she does. Soaphead closes his letter and thinks lovingly about all the miscellaneous objects he has collected. He is asleep when his landlord discovers her dead dog.

ANALYSIS

Like Geraldine and Pauline, Soaphead Church is another example of how the worship of whiteness and cleanliness can deform a black life. His mixed blood gives him a false sense of superiority, which he maintains with delusions of grandeur. Indeed, he half-convinces himself that he can work miracles and that he has a direct line to God. His disgust at human physicality leaves him isolated and lonely and leads him to direct his sexual impulses toward young girls. The narrator ironically describes him as "a very clean old man" instead of a dirty old man, and the implication is clear: his obsession with bodily purity has made him more perverted than simple lust would have.

While Pauline and Cholly are described with sympathy despite their many flaws, Soaphead Church is more of a parody than a multidimensional character. He is labeled as a type, a misanthrope (or people-hater) who prefers objects to people. The narrator comments ironically that like many misanthropes, Soaphead chooses a career that puts him in direct, intimate contact with people. When

Soaphead is given the chance to narrate his own story, in his letter to God, he is not made more sympathetic, as Pauline is when she narrates her story. Instead, he becomes still more absurd, using pretentious and frequently melodramatic language, blaming God for his own failings, and justifying himself with hypocritical claims of good and pure intentions. He writes in ridiculously precise and detailed prose, saying of his claim to possess God's power that "it was not a complete *lie*; but it was a *complete* lie," as if there were a meaningful difference between the two.

Soaphead's hypocrisy is made all the more venomous by the fact that he is well-educated. Labeling himself a "misanthrope" and reading the writings of other misanthropes make him feel as if his behavior is somehow acceptable and even intellectually justified. When he reads works of literature, he remembers the parts that reinforce his own predilections and ignores the parts that challenge them. His hypocrisy is also associated with his religious pretension—his false claim to know God's will even though it is clear to those in the ministry that he does not have a genuine spiritual calling. Much like Pauline's religious sense of martyrdom, Soaphead's relationship with God is an indirect way to express frustration with his life. As a general rule, the religious characters in this novel tend to be the least loving. Soaphead Church is the most extreme example of loveless religiosity.

Soaphead is made into a parody not only to make obvious to us that he is a bad person. Through his character, Morrison also wishes to critique yet another deceptive method of dealing with racial self-hatred. While education may seem to be an escape, the Western education that Soaphead's family has received reinforces and even exaggerates their self-denial and perversity. While religion may be an escape, it also promotes self-denial and encourages a dangerous, delusional self-righteousness. True freedom and happiness, Morrison suggests, come from a feeling of connectedness with one's own body, not a denial of it.

SUMMER: CHAPTER 10

Nobody paid us any attention, so we paid very good attention to ourselves. Our limitations were not known to us—not then.　　(See QUOTATIONS, p. 53)

SUMMARY
Summer arrives, a time of storms. Claudia remembers a storm her mother told her about that blew away half of South Lorain in 1929. She imagines her mother being pulled up into the air, smiling with her hand on her hip, unconcerned. Frieda and Claudia are selling marigold seeds to earn money for a new bicycle. Even though their mother has told them only to visit houses they know, they tromp all over town. When they are invited in at homes they know to refresh themselves with a cold drink, they overhear adult conversations and begin to piece together a story about Pecola.

Claudia and Frieda learn that Pecola has been impregnated by her father. Cholly has now run away. The neighborhood gossips are disgusted by Cholly's action but also blame Pecola. They think she should be taken out of school. When her mother found her, she beat her almost to death. The gossips think that it would be best for the unborn baby to die. Claudia and Frieda are embarrassed and hurt for Pecola, and their sorrow is intensified by the fact that none of the adults seems to share it. Claudia can picture the baby in the womb, with beautiful eyes, lips, and skin. She thinks that wanting Pecola's baby to live is a way to counteract everyone else's love of white dolls and white little girls. She and Frieda are unconcerned with the incestuous component of the story—they do not understand how babies are made in the first place.

Claudia and Frieda decide to help Pecola by praying and by giving a sacrifice; they will give up their seed money and plant the rest of the marigold seeds. They will bury the money by Pecola's house and bury the seeds in their own yard so that they can tend them. Claudia will sing and Frieda will say the magic words.

ANALYSIS
This chapter juxtaposes a variety of different ways of understanding and telling stories. In Claudia's opening discussion of storms, she distinguishes "public fact" from "private reality." It is a public fact that a tornado destroyed part of Lorain in the summer of 1929, but

Claudia's image of her mother floating in this storm is a dream image cast by the complexity of her private reality. Storms to her are not simple facts; they are connected in her mind to the texture of strawberries, dust, darkness, and the sticky feeling of humidity. Paradoxically, they are both frightening and satisfying. Her memory of a summer storm gets mixed up with the story her mother has told about the tornado, demonstrating that "public facts" are made private not only because of the personal connotations they hold for individuals, but also because they are distorted by memory. The image of her mother she conjures—strong, smiling, unconcerned by the storm even when it lifts her into the air—has less to do with the reality of storms than with her own admiration for her mother's beauty, toughness, and independence. Her mother is a source of stability in the midst of metaphorical and real storms.

At the same time, Pecola's story is both a matter of public fact and private reality. No one tells Claudia and Frieda the story directly or explains to them what it means. They are given the burden and the freedom of deciding for themselves what it means. They resist what they understand from the adults' narrative, which implicates Pecola in Cholly's "nastiness" and dismisses the entire family as crazy and ugly. Claudia and Frieda listen carefully, but they never hear sympathy or concern in the adults' dialogue. Claudia tells herself a separate story that will include the sympathy she feels: the baby is beautiful inside the womb, much more beautiful than white dolls. She and Frieda, fearless at that age, cast themselves as heroines in a story that looks toward the baby's future instead of back at the ugliness of its creation. Pecola's baby must live, and they must save it.

They decide that, to save the baby, they must make a miracle. This miracle is to work by metaphorical rather than practical logic. First, they will petition God, but they suspect that a petition is powerful only if it is accompanied by the genuine sacrifice of their hard-earned money and seeds. Claudia and Frieda's plan is not practical, of course, and it does not work. But their plan permits them to imagine a world in which human beings are connected to one another and to nature. They imagine that their sacrifice can earn Pecola's safety and that the fruitfulness of the earth will parallel the fruitfulness of Pecola. Most of all, they imagine that words and song can be healing. Their hopefulness is a symbol of the hopefulness of the novel as a whole, which attempts to heal the terribly disjointed community it describes by lyrically telling its story.

SUMMER: CHAPTER 11

*All of our waste which we dumped on her and which
she absorbed. And all of our beauty, which was hers
first and which she gave to us.*

(See QUOTATIONS, p. 54)

SUMMARY

Two voices are in dialogue: Pecola and an imaginary friend, whose voice is in italics. The friend criticizes Pecola for looking in the mirror constantly, but Pecola cannot stop admiring her new blue eyes. The imaginary friend wants to go out and play, and Pecola accuses her of being jealous. Pecola agrees to go outside, however, and brags that she can look at the sun without blinking. Pecola tells her friend that now that she has blue eyes, no one looks at her, not even her mother. She thinks they are jealous. Pecola wonders why the imaginary friend has not come before, and the friend tells her that she did not need her before. Pecola explains that she no longer goes to school because people are prejudiced against her blue eyes. She asks her friend if her eyes are the very bluest, and her friend reassures her. She asks her imaginary friend where she lives, and the friend rebuffs her. Pecola worries that her mother does not see her new friend.

The imaginary friend begins talking about Cholly. She speculates that Mrs. Breedlove must miss him. She observes that they had sex a lot, but Pecola counters that he made her do it. The friend says that Cholly made Pecola do it as well, and Pecola denies this. The friend reminds Pecola that Cholly raped her again while she was reading on the couch. Pecola explains that she did not tell her mother because her mother did not believe her the first time. Now both Cholly and Sammy are gone for good. The friend implies that Pecola enjoyed Cholly's sexual advances the second time, and Pecola gets angry. They decide to return to the topic of her eyes. Pecola worries that someone somewhere may have bluer eyes than she. She wants her friend to examine everyone's eyes to see if they are bluer than hers. She wonders if her eyes are "blue enough" but cannot say blue enough for what. The friend tells her she is being silly and temporarily departs.

Claudia begins to narrate and describes Pecola's madness. Pecola wanders the street jerking her arms as if trying to fly. Claudia and Frieda feel like failures because their flowers never grow and Pecola's baby is prematurely stillborn. Cholly dies in a workhouse, and Pecola and Mrs. Breedlove move to a house on the edge of town. Claudia feels that the town has dumped all its garbage upon Pecola, and all her beauty. Pecola's ugliness allowed all the others to believe they were beautiful, healthy, and sanctified. Claudia feels herself to be no better than the others and implicates herself in using Pecola as a scapegoat. She believes that the Maginot Line and Cholly loved Pecola but that love is only as good as the lover, and therefore Cholly's love killed her. It is too easy simply to blame the climate of the town as inhospitable to certain kinds of people or flowers. In any case, in the final words of Claudia, "it's much, much, much too late."

> *Wicked people love wickedly, violent people love*
> *violently, weak people love weakly, stupid people love*
> *stupidly, but the love of a free man is never safe.*
> (See QUOTATIONS, p. 61)

ANALYSIS

When Pecola is finally granted her wish for blue eyes, she receives it in a perverse and darkly ironic form. She is able to obtain blue eyes only by losing her mind. Rather than granting Pecola insight into the world around her and providing a redeeming connection with other people, these eyes are a form of blindness. Pecola can no longer accurately perceive the outside world, and she has become even more invisible to others. Pecola has managed to write a new narrative about her life, an act that is sometimes healing for other characters in the novel, but this narrative reinforces her isolation from the world rather than reconnects her to it. Her new friendship is only imagined and does not protect her from old suffering or insecurity. She is worried by the fact that others will not look at her, and she has not escaped her jealousy of what others possess—she worries that someone has bluer eyes than she. Her belief in her blue eyes is not enough, and she requires constant reassurance. As is made abundantly clear when the imaginary friend brings up the painful subject of Cholly, Pecola has not escaped her demons. She has merely recast them in a new form.

The closing section of the novel is written in the first person plural, and Claudia does not permit herself any escape from her vivid and total criticism of the community. This is somewhat surprising, given Claudia and Frieda's efforts to save Pecola's baby by sacrificing money and marigold seeds. Nevertheless, looking back, Claudia understands that Pecola has been a scapegoat—someone the community could use to exorcise its own self-hatred by expressing that hatred toward her. She explains that Pecola's ugliness gave the community, herself included, a false sense of beauty: "We were so beautiful when we stood astride her ugliness." Moreover, Pecola's suffering made the community feel comparatively happy, and her failure to speak for herself allowed them to feel articulate. This last criticism leads us to question Claudia's reliability as a narrator. It is possible that her version of Pecola's story is secretly self-serving and that the true meaning of Pecola's life remains unexplained.

Just as the novel begins with two prologues, perhaps the best way to think of the ending of *The Bluest Eye* is to understand it as two endings. The first ending, the close of the previous chapter, is a hopeful one: Claudia and Frieda selflessly sacrifice their own desires to help Pecola, planting seeds to suggest that nature always promises rebirth, saying magic words and singing to suggest that lyrical language can redeem a fractured life. The second ending is a despairing one: Claudia too is capable of selfishly using Pecola to reinforce her own sense of worth, the earth is cruel, and, in any case, nature cannot redeem human failings. The book closes on this second, bleak vision. But the lyric beauty of Morrison's language, which picks up momentum in this final section, suggests that there may be a kind of redemption in remembering, in telling stories, and in singing, after all.

Important Quotations Explained

1. "It never occurred to either of us that the earth itself
    might have been unyielding. We had dropped our
    seeds in our own little plot of black dirt just as
    Pecola's father had dropped his seeds in his own plot
    of black dirt. Our innocence and faith were no more
    productive than his lust or despair."

This quotation is from the second prologue to the novel, in which
Claudia anticipates the events that the novel will recount, most
notably Pecola's pregnancy by incest. Here, she remembers that she
and Frieda blamed each other for the failure of the marigolds to
grow one summer, but now she wonders if the earth itself was hostile to them—a darker, more radical possibility. The idea of blame is
important because the book continually raises the question of who
is to blame for Pecola's suffering. Are Claudia and Frieda at fault for
not doing more to help Pecola? To some degree, we can blame
Pecola's suffering on her parents and on racism; but Cholly and
Pauline have themselves suffered, and the causes of suffering seem
so diffuse and prevalent that it seems possible that life on earth itself
is hostile to human happiness. This hostility is what the earth's hostility to the marigolds represents. The complexity of the question of
blame increases when Claudia makes the stunning parallel between
the healing action of their planting of the marigold seeds and
Cholly's hurtful action of raping Pecola. Claudia suggests that the
impulse that drove her and her sister and the impulse that drove
Cholly might not be so different after all. Motives of innocence and
faith seem to be no more effective than motives of lust and despair in
the universe of the novel.

2.　It had occurred to Pecola some time ago that if her
　　eyes, those eyes that held the pictures, and knew the
　　sights—if those eyes of hers were different, that is to
　　say, beautiful, she herself would be different.

These lines, which introduce Pecola's desire for blue eyes, are found
in Chapter 3 of the "Autumn" section of the novel. They demon-
strate the complexity of Pecola's desire—she does not want blue
eyes simply because they conform to white beauty standards, but
because she wishes to possess different sights and pictures, as if
changing eye color will change reality. Pecola has just been forced to
witness a violent fight between her parents, and the only solution
she can imagine to her passive suffering is to witness something different. She believes that if she had blue eyes, their beauty would
inspire beautiful and kindly behavior on the part of others. Pecola's
desire has its own logic even if it is naïve. To Pecola, the color of
one's skin and eyes do influence how one is treated and what one is
forced to witness.

3. We had defended ourselves since memory against
    everything and everybody, considered all speech a
    code to be broken by us, and all gestures subject to
    careful analysis; we had become headstrong, devious,
    and arrogant. Nobody paid us any attention, so we
    paid very good attention to ourselves. Our limitations
    were not known to us—not then.

This quotation is from Claudia, and it occurs in the second-to-last chapter of the novel. It can be read as a concise description of Claudia and Frieda's ethos as a whole. The MacTeer girls take an active stance against whatever they perceive threatens them, whether it is a white doll, boys making fun of Pecola, Henry's molestation of Frieda, or the community's rejection of Pecola. Their active and energetic responses contrast sharply with Pecola's passive suffering. Though Claudia and Frieda's actions are childish and often doomed to failure, they are still examples of vigorous responses to oppression. Claudia hints here, however, that this willingness to take action no matter who defies them disappears with adulthood. Frieda and Claudia are able to be active in part because they are protected by their parents, and in part because they do not confront the life-or-death problems that Pecola does. As adults, they will learn to respond to antagonism in more indirect and perhaps more self-destructive ways.

QUOTATIONS

4.   The birdlike gestures are worn away to a mere picking
      and plucking her way between the tire rims and the
      sunflowers, between Coke bottles and milkweed,
      among all the waste and beauty of the world—which
      is what she herself was. All of our waste which we
      dumped on her and which she absorbed. And all of
      our beauty, which was hers first and which she gave
      to us.

This quotation, from the last chapter of the novel, sums up Claudia's impressions of Pecola's madness. Here, she transforms Pecola into a symbol of the beauty and suffering that marks all human life and into a more specific symbol of the hopes and fears of her community. The community has dumped all of its "waste" on Pecola because she is a convenient scapegoat. The blackness and ugliness that the other members of the community fear reside in themselves can instead be attributed to her. But Claudia also describes Pecola as the paragon of beauty, a startling claim after all the emphasis on Pecola's ugliness. Pecola is beautiful because she is human, but this beauty is invisible to the members of the community who have identified beauty with whiteness. She gives others beauty because their assumptions about her ugliness make them feel beautiful in comparison. In this sense, Pecola's gift of beauty is ironic—she gives people beauty because they think she is ugly, not because they perceive her true beauty as a human being.

5.   Love is never any better than the lover. Wicked people
love wickedly, violent people love violently, weak
people love weakly, stupid people love stupidly, but
the love of a free man is never safe. There is no gift for
the beloved. The lover alone possesses his gift of love.
The loved one is shorn, neutralized, frozen in the glare
of the lover's inward eye.

This quotation is from the last chapter of the novel, in which Claudia attempts to tell us what her story means. It describes love as a
potentially damaging force, following the suggestion that Cholly
was the only person who loved Pecola "enough to touch her." If
love and rape cannot be distinguished, then we have entered a world
in which love itself is ambiguous. Against the usual idea that love is
inherently healing and redemptive, Claudia suggests that love is
only as good as the lover. This is why the broken, warped human
beings in this novel fail to love one another well. In fact, Claudia
suggests, love may even be damaging, because it locks the loved one
in a potentially destructive gaze. Romantic love creates a damaging
demand for beauty—the kind of beauty that black girls, by defini-
tion, may never be able to possess because of the racist standards of
their society. But the pessimism of this passage is offset by the inherent hopefulness of the idea of love. If we can understand Cholly's
behavior as driven by love as well as anger (and his rape of Pecola is
in fact described in these terms), then there is still some good in him,
however deformed. We are left to hope for a kind of love that is a
genuine gift for the beloved.

QUOTATIONS

KEY FACTS

FULL TITLE
The Bluest Eye

AUTHOR
Toni Morrison

TYPE OF WORK
Novel

GENRE
Coming-of-age, tragedy, elegy

LANGUAGE
English

TIME AND PLACE WRITTEN
New York, 1962–1965

DATE OF FIRST PUBLICATION
1970

PUBLISHER
Holt, Rinehart, and Winston. The novel went out of print in 1974 but was later rereleased.

NARRATOR
There are two narrators: Claudia MacTeer, who narrates in a mixture of a child's and an adult's perspective; and an omniscient narrator.

POINT OF VIEW
Claudia's and Pecola's points of view are dominant, but we also see things from Cholly's, Pauline's, and other characters' points of view. Point of view is deliberately fragmented to give a sense of the characters' experiences of dislocation and to help us sympathize with multiple characters.

TONE
Lyrical, elegiac, embittered, matter-of-fact, colloquial

TENSE
Past, as seen by the adult Claudia

SETTING (TIME)
1940–1941

SETTING (PLACE)
Lorain, Ohio

PROTAGONIST
Pecola Breedlove

MAJOR CONFLICT
Pecola needs to receive love from somebody, but her parents
and the other members of her community are unable to love
her because they have been damaged and thwarted in their
own lives.

RISING ACTION
Cholly tries to burn down the family house; Pecola is snubbed
by a grocer, tormented by boys, and blamed for killing a cat.

CLIMAX
Pecola's father rapes her.

FALLING ACTION
Pecola is beaten by her mother, requests blue eyes from
Soaphead Church, begins to go mad, and loses her baby.

THEMES
Whiteness as the standard of beauty; seeing versus being seen;
the power of stories; sexual initiation and abuse; satisfying
appetites versus repressing them

MOTIFS
The Dick-and-Jane narrative; the seasons and nature; whiteness
and color; eyes and vision; dirtiness and cleanliness

SYMBOLS
The house; bluest eyes; the marigolds

FORESHADOWING
The prologue foreshadows the major events of the plot.

KEY FACTS

STUDY QUESTIONS &
ESSAY TOPICS

STUDY QUESTIONS

1. *The Bluest Eye uses multiple narrators, including Claudia as a child, Claudia as an adult, and an omniscient narrator. Which narrative point of view do you think is most central to the novel and why?*

A case can be made for the centrality of any of the three narrators listed above. The perspective of the adult Claudia frames the novel—the second section of the prologue and the novel's last chapter are told from her point of view. These opening and closing sections say the most about what Pecola's story means, and our efforts to make sense of the story therefore depend upon and parallel the adult Claudia's efforts. But Claudia's childlike perspective is also crucial. She is similar to Pecola in age and social status, and therefore possesses special insight into the nature and meaning of Pecola's suffering. At the same time, she is comparatively more confident and secure than Pecola, so she can articulate things that Pecola cannot. The omniscient narrator is also central to the telling of the story, because she provides information about Cholly's and Pauline's pasts, which make them more sympathetic and give the novel its broader scope. Without the character backgrounds provided by this omniscient perspective, Pecola's tragedy might be too senseless for the novel to hold together.

2. *Who do you think is the most sympathetic character in the novel and why?*

Morrison designs *The Bluest Eye* to make us sympathize with even the most violent and hurtful characters, which means that this question has many possible answers. Pecola is the most obvious candidate for our sympathy, because she undergoes a shocking amount of abuse. She is forced to witness her parents' violent fights, she is mocked or ignored by her classmates, she is tormented by Junior, she is raped by her father, and she is used by Soaphead Church. But to some degree, Pecola remains a shadowy, mysterious character— we are not given as much insight into how she thinks and feels as we are into other characters, who may therefore receive the greater share of our sympathy. Both of Pecola's parents are sympathetic because the narrator goes to great lengths to explain how they have become the kind of people they are. Pauline's story is partially narrated by Pauline herself, which makes her more sympathetic because we are given a vivid glimpse into the pleasure and suffering of her life. Although Cholly does not narrate any part of his story, he endures so much hardship—starting from the moment he is born and discarded by the train tracks—that we cannot help but feel sympathy for him. Claudia is yet another candidate for the most sympathetic character, simply because we experience so much of the story from her point of view and she is the one who helps us makes sense of it all.

3.   The Bluest Eye *is a novel about racism, and yet there are relatively few instances of the direct oppression of black people by white people in the book. Explain how racism functions in the story.*

Unlike *To Kill a Mockingbird,* in which an African-American is persecuted by whites simply on the basis of skin color, *The Bluest Eye* presents a more complicated portrayal of racism. The characters do experience direct oppression, but more routinely they are subject to an internalized set of values that creates its own cycle of victimization within families and the neighborhood. The black community in the novel has accepted white standards of beauty, judging Maureen's light skin to be attractive and Pecola's dark skin to be ugly. Claudia can sense the destructiveness of this idea and rebels against it when she destroys her white doll and imagines Pecola's unborn baby as beautiful. Racism also affects the characters of the novel in other indirect ways. The general sense of precariousness of the black community during the Great Depression, in comparison with the relative affluence of the whites in the novel, reminds us of the link between race and class. More directly, the sexual violation of Pecola is connected to the sexual violation of Cholly by whites who view his loss of virginity as entertainment.

QUESTIONS & ESSAYS

SUGGESTED ESSAY TOPICS

1. How does nature function in the novel? Do you consider it a benevolent presence against which the events of the novel are contrasted, or a potentially malevolent force? Is Morrison's use of natural imagery hopeful or ironic?

2. Which is a greater threat to the children in *The Bluest Eye*: racism or sexism?

3. At the end of the novel, Claudia questions her own right or ability to tell the truth about Pecola's experience. How seriously are we to take her questioning? Is she a reliable narrator?

4. To what extent is Cholly to blame for his violence against his family? Which other people or circumstances may also be to blame? What is the novel's position on blame?

5. The novel includes a number of secondary story lines, such as Geraldine's and Soaphead Church's histories, with the main story line of the Breedlove family. Select one of these secondary stories and explain how it relates to or comments upon the main story line.

REVIEW & RESOURCES

QUIZ

1. Which of the following is a distinguishing characteristic of Pauline Breedlove?

    A. She has blue eyes
    B. She has a bad foot
    C. She has a curved spine
    D. She is balding

2. Why does Pecola stay briefly with the MacTeers?

    A. Her father has raped her
    B. She has run away from home
    C. Her father has tried to burn down their home
    D. She is visiting her friends Claudia and Frieda

3. Who lives above the Breedloves' apartment?

    A. Three prostitutes
    B. Henry Washington
    C. Soaphead Church
    D. The MacTeers

4. Where does Mrs. Breedlove work?

    A. At a restaurant
    B. At the local school
    C. At the home of a white family
    D. At the MacTeers' home

5. What important event occurs when Pecola is staying with the Breedloves?

    A. She kills the family cat
    B. She is molested by Henry Washington
    C. She poisons the family dog
    D. She menstruates for the first time

6. Who hates white baby dolls?

    A.   Frieda
    B.   Claudia
    C.   Pecola
    D.   Maureen Peal

7. Who raises Cholly?

    A.   Aunt Jimmy
    B.   M'Dear
    C.   His violent father
    D.   Blue Jack

8. Which of the following characters is still alive when the story ends?

    A.   Cholly
    B.   Pecola's baby
    C.   Pauline Breedlove
    D.   Aunt Jimmy

9. What flowers do Claudia and Frieda plant to save Pecola's baby?

    A.   Roses
    B.   Dandelions
    C.   Marigolds
    D.   Lilacs

10. Where does most of the action in the novel take place?

    A.   Princeton, Kentucky
    B.   Crossville, Tennessee
    C.   Macon, Georgia
    D.   Lorain, Ohio

11. Which of the following does *not* happen to Pecola after her father rapes her?

    A.   Her father rapes her a second time
    B.   She runs away with a local man
    C.   She becomes pregnant
    D.   She goes mad

12. In what way is Pecola's wish for blue eyes fulfilled at the end of the story?

   A. She develops an eye disease that turns them blue
   B. She uses dye to make them blue and goes blind
   C. She comes to believe that she has blue eyes
   D. Everyone else tells her she has blue eyes

13. What happens when Cholly finds his father?

   A. He is frightened by his father's manner and runs away
   B. His father disowns him
   C. His father tries to beat him up
   D. His father embraces him

14. What happens after Aunt Jimmy's funeral?

   A. Cholly beats up a younger boy
   B. Cholly has sex for the first time
   C. Cholly becomes ill
   D. Cholly kills three white men

15. Who takes refuge in the movies?

   A. Claudia
   B. Pecola
   C. Pauline Breedlove
   D. Sammy

16. What happens to Sammy at the end of the story?

   A. He runs away for good
   B. He attempts to kill his father
   C. He helps Pecola escape
   D. He is beaten by his mother

17. Whose cat is Pecola blamed for killing?

   A. Mrs. MacTeer's
   B. The Maginot Line's
   C. Her mother's
   D. Geraldine's

REVIEW & RESOURCES

18. What is Pauline doing when she meets Cholly?

    A. Doing the laundry
    B. Standing in the garden
    C. Auditioning for a movie role
    D. Fighting with her first husband

19. Who temporarily befriends Pecola after Pecola is teased by a group of boys?

    A. Rosemary Villanucci
    B. Claudia MacTeer
    C. Junior
    D. Maureen Peal

20. Why does Henry Washington send Claudia and Frieda out for ice cream?

    A. So that he can steal from Mrs. MacTeer
    B. So that he can drink all of Mrs. MacTeer's milk
    C. So that he can entertain prostitutes
    D. So that his Bible-study group can meet in peace

21. What kind of pets does Junior have?

    A. A cat and kittens
    B. A dog and puppies
    C. A frog and tadpoles
    D. A duck and ducklings

22. What is peculiar about Maureen Peal's hands?

    A. There are only four fingers on each hand
    B. There are scars where she was burned as a child
    C. There are stumps where her sixth fingers
        were removed
    D. Her thumbs are double-jointed

23. Why does Mrs. Breedlove have a limp?

    A. She broke her hip when she fell down a flight of stairs
    B. She impaled her foot on a nail as a child
    C. One of her legs is shorter than the other
    D. She has arthritis in her right leg

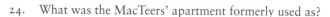

24. What was the MacTeers' apartment formerly used as?

    A. A hospital clinic
    B. A storage room
    C. A hotel room
    D. A store

25. What is Soaphead Church's occupation?

    A. A doctor
    B. A dream interpreter
    C. A preacher
    D. A scholar

ANSWER KEY:
1: B; 2: C; 3: A; 4: C; 5: D; 6: B; 7: A; 8: C; 9: C; 10: D;
11: B; 12: C; 13: A; 14: B; 15: C; 16: A; 17: D; 18: B; 19: D;
20: C; 21: A; 22: C; 23: B; 24: D; 25: B

SUGGESTIONS FOR FURTHER READING

BOUSON, J. BROOKS. *Quiet As It's Kept: Shame, Trauma, and Race in the Novels of Toni Morrison.* Albany: State University of New York Press, 2000.

CONNER, MARC C., ed. *The Aesthetics of Toni Morrison: Speaking the Unspeakable.* Jackson: University Press of Mississippi, 2000.

DAVID, RON. *Toni Morrison Explained: A Reader's Road Map to the Novels.* New York: Random House, 2000.

GATES, HENRY LOUIS and K. A. APPIAH, ed. *Toni Morrison: Critical Perspectives Past and Present.* New York: Amistad, 1993.

KUBITSCHEK, MISSY DEHN. *Toni Morrison: A Critical Companion.* Westport, Connecticut: Greenwood Press, 1998.

MORRISON, TONI. *Conversations with Toni Morrison.* Ed. Danille Taylor-Guthrie. Jackson: University Press of Mississippi, 1994.

PETERSON, NANCY J., ed. *Toni Morrison: Critical and Theoretical Approaches.* Baltimore: Johns Hopkins University Press, 1997.

RICE, HERBERT WILLIAM. *Toni Morrison and the American Tradition: A Rhetorical Reading.* New York: Peter Lang, 1996.

REVIEW & RESOURCES

A Note on the Type

The typeface used in SparkNotes study guides is Sabon, created by master typographer Jan Tschichold in 1964. Tschichold revolutionized the field of graphic design twice: first with his use of asymmetrical layouts and sanserif type in the 1930s when he was affiliated with the Bauhaus, then by abandoning assymetry and calling for a return to the classic ideals of design. Sabon, his only extant typeface, is emblematic of his latter program: Tschichold's design is a recreation of the types made by Claude Garamond, the great French typographer of the Renaissance, and his contemporary Robert Granjon. Fittingly, it is named for Garamond's apprentice, Jacques Sabon.

SPARKNOTES
TEST PREPARATION
GUIDES

The SparkNotes team figured it was time to cut standardized tests down to size. We've studied the tests for you, so that SparkNotes test prep guides are:

Smarter:
Packed with critical-thinking skills and test-
taking strategies that will improve your score.

Better:
Fully up to date, covering all new features of the tests,
with study tips on every type of question.

Faster:
Our books cover exactly what you need to
know for the test. No more, no less.

SparkNotes Guide to the SAT & PSAT
SparkNotes Guide to the SAT & PSAT—Deluxe Internet Edition
SparkNotes Guide to the ACT
SparkNotes Guide to the ACT—Deluxe Internet Edition
SparkNotes Guide to the SAT II Writing
SparkNotes Guide to the SAT II U.S. History
SparkNotes Guide to the SAT II Math Ic
SparkNotes Guide to the SAT II Math IIc
SparkNotes Guide to the SAT II Biology
SparkNotes Guide to the SAT II Physics

SAT and PSAT are registered trademarks of the College Entrance Examination Board, which does not endorse these books.
ACT is a registered trademark of ACT, Inc. which neither sponsors nor endorses these books.

SparkNotes Literature Guides